V

D0794627

THRILL SEEKERS

SKYDIVING

BY HEATHER MOORE NIVER

Gareth Stevens
Publishing

Please visit our website, www.garethstevens.com. For a free color catalog of all our high-quality books, call toll free 1-800-542-2595 or fax 1-877-542-2596.

Library of Congress Cataloging-in-Publication Data

Niver, Heather Moore.
Skydiving / by Heather Moore Niver.
  p. cm. — (Thrill seekers)
Includes index.
ISBN 978-1-4824-3293-0 (pbk.)
ISBN 978-1-4339-9918-5 (6-pack)
ISBN 978-1-4339-9916-1 (library binding)
1. Skydiving — Juvenile literature. I. Niver, Heather Moore. II. Title.
GV770.N58 2014
797.5—dc23

First Edition

Published in 2014 by
Gareth Stevens Publishing
111 East 14th Street, Suite 349
New York, NY 10003

Copyright © 2014 Gareth Stevens Publishing

Designer: Michael J. Flynn
Editor: Therese Shea

Photo credits: Cover, p. 1 Digital Vision/Getty Images; pp. 5, 10, 11, 13, 18 Germanskydiver/Shutterstock.com;
p. 7 (main) Xavier Rossi/Gamma-Rapho/Getty Images; p. 7 (sketch) Omikron/Photo Researchers/Shutterstock.com;
p. 7 (paper) saiva/Shutterstock.com; p. 9 Jerry-Rainey/Shutterstock.com; p. 15 Victor Decolongon/Getty Images;
p. 17 (main) Vitalii Nesterchuk/Shutterstock.com; p. 17 (inset) Sahani Photography/Shutterstock.com;
p. 19 Christof Koepsel/Bongarts/Getty Images; p. 21 Thinkstock Images/Comstock Images/Getty Images;
p. 23 Rick Neves/Shutterstock.com; p. 24 http://en.wikipedia.org/wiki/File:Joseph_Kittinger,_Jr.jpg;
p. 25 http://en.wikipedia.org/wiki/File:Kittinger-jump.jpg; p. 27 Jay Nemos/Red Bull Stratos/AP Photo;
p. 29 Lobo Press/Peter Arnold/Getty Images.

Printed in the United States of America

CPSIA compliance information: Batch #CW14GS: For further information contact Gareth Stevens, New York, New York at 1-800-542-2595.

CONTENTS

Words in the glossary appear in **bold** type
the first time they are used in the text.

FALLING FAST FOR FUN

Sure, **parachutes** are handy when you need to leap from an airplane headed for a crash, but who jumps out of a plane for fun? Lots of people do and love it! Skydiving has become a popular sport.

Skydivers may fall through the air at about 120 miles (193 km) per hour, so they really love speed. Some people jump once or twice for fun. Others go skydiving hundreds and even thousands of times in their lives! A few skydivers are so skilled that they take part in competitions. All skydiving requires safety and training, though.

First Skydive?

The first skydive may have occurred in ancient China, or at least one legend makes it sound like it. Emperor Shun ruled China between 2258 BC and 2208 BC. A tale says that he escaped a fiery tower by tying several cone-shaped straw hats together. The hats worked as a parachute, and he landed safely!

Skydiving is one of the ultimate thrills for seekers of adventure.

EARLY JUMPS

Once Wilbur and Orville Wright got their airplane off the ground in 1903, the parachute became an important safety tool. Historians disagree about who made the first official skydive, but many think it was Grant Morton. In 1911, he jumped from a Wright Model B airplane flying over Venice Beach, California, and used a silk parachute to safely reach the ground.

After World War II (1939–1945), paratroopers, or soldiers trained to go to battle by parachute, found they missed the thrill of the jump. They used their experiences to start jumping for fun. Soon, skydiving started to become popular for others, too.

Da Vinci's Design

In 1483, famous artist and inventor Leonardo da Vinci drew pyramid-shaped parachutes made out of cloth and wooden poles. He wrote: "If a man is provided with a length of **gummed** linen cloth with a length of 12 yards on each side and 12 yards high, he can jump from any great height whatsoever without injury."

This is Leonardo da Vinci's design for a parachute as well as a model of what it would look like.

READY, SET, JUMP!

Before a skydive, jumpers start out by packing and checking their own parachutes. Then they dress in a special jumpsuit. Jumpers often double-check each other's straps and **rig** to make sure everything is correctly fastened.

Now it's time to board the plane. There might be as many as 20 other jumpers on board. The plane flies up to an ideal **altitude**, which is usually about 13,000 feet (3,962 m). At this height, a skydiver can look forward to about 60 seconds of **free fall** before opening their parachute. When the plane is in the right position, it's time to jump!

Perfecting Parachutes

In the early 1900s, parachutes for skydiving were sometimes inflated before a jump. Other times, a skydiver jumped off a platform, pulling a parachute out of a box and into the air. The uninflated jump wasn't safe, so the **rip cord** was invented. It wasn't used much until the 1920s, though.

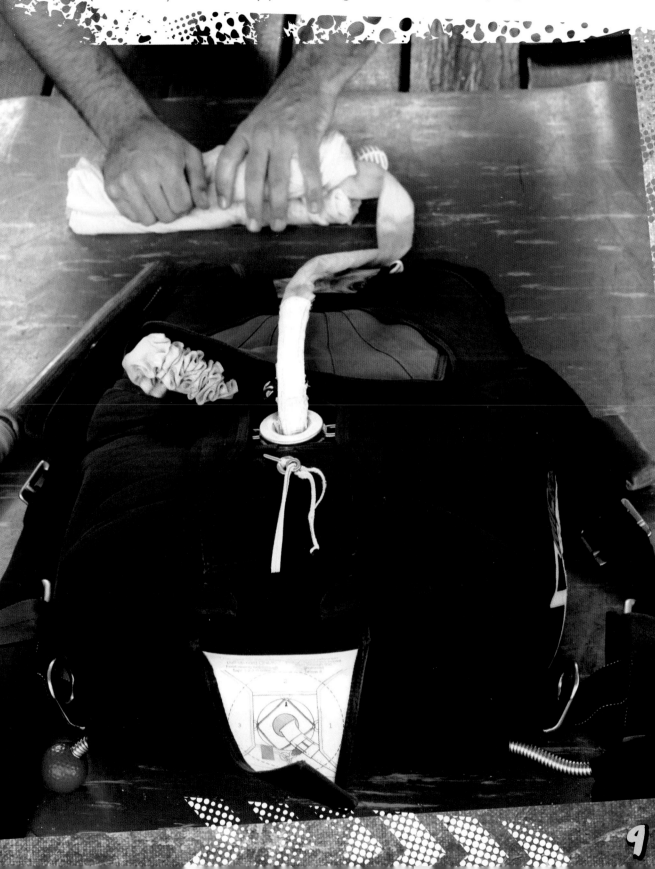

A skydiver carefully packs his rig before he takes the plunge.

A person's first skydive is usually a tandem jump. That means a jumper is strapped to an instructor, or jumpmaster, for the dive. The jumpmaster wears a giant parachute to handle the weight.

As the two jump from the plane, the jumpmaster throws out a **drogue** (DROHG). The drogue slows down the falling pair. Without it, the two divers would drop 180 to 200 miles (290 to 322 km) per hour. Even with the drogue, they plunge at about 120 miles (193 km) per hour! The instructor or the student pulls the rip cord, the parachute is released, and the pair land together safely.

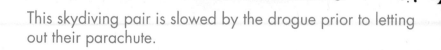

This skydiving pair is slowed by the drogue prior to letting out their parachute.

On a tandem skydive, the instructor is in control of everything, so skydivers can experience the jump without worrying.

Tandem Isn't Tame!

Tandem jumping might sound tame, but you can ask your jumpmaster to do special turns and flips in the air. You drop through the air without a chute for about 1 minute. When the chute opens, you jerk back upward about three stories in just 10 seconds!

ACCELERATED FREE FALL

People who want more than just a tandem jump might want to become **licensed** skydivers. One way to do this is the accelerated free fall (AFF) method. First, jumpers need several hours of ground instruction. Then, they start jumping. However, two instructors jump with them and tell them how to move and turn through the whole dive using hand signals and radios.

In the United States, accelerated free fall includes seven levels of training in all. After the first few levels, depending on their progress, jumpers might jump without being attached to an instructor. On level seven, though, AFF skydivers jump on their own!

Past Parachutes

Another early story of parachuting took place in China in the 1100s. A thief escaped with gold by parachuting to safety using two umbrellas. Chinese and Thai acrobats may have used umbrellas as parachutes while doing stunts. Their acts may have inspired the first European parachute in the 1680s.

AFF is called "accelerated" because it's the fastest way to learn free-fall skills.

DIVING IN THE DARK

For an even more extreme experience, some skydivers jump at night. The challenge is greater because it's easy to become confused in the dark. Landmarks on the ground can be hard to see, and it's also hard to tell how near or far things are.

A clear, moonlit night is best for a night dive, but moonlight can also make the jumper's shadow look like another skydiver! Night skydivers often do several daytime jumps in the place where they want to jump so they know the area well.

Why would they do something so risky? Imagine seeing city lights from above. The view can be breathtaking!

Surf the Sky

Skysurfers skydive with a sky surfboard and land with a parachute. During free fall, they spin, twist, and slide through the air. A cameraflyer often jumps, too, to take video of the jump with the camera strapped to their helmet. In competitions, both jumpers are judged for their creativity and athletics.

Every skydiver wants a safe landing, so they can go on to try another heart-pounding skydive!

BASE JUMPING

Jumping out of a plane isn't daring enough for some people, so they try something riskier: BASE jumping. "BASE" stands for buildings, **antennas**, spans (bridges), and Earth (natural formations). Jumping from these places is incredibly dangerous. The smallest mistake can mean serious injury or death. Most BASE jumpers have made about 100 skydive jumps before BASE jumping.

BASE jumpers use rectangular parachutes, called ram-air parachutes, which can be more easily controlled than skydiving parachutes. BASE jumping starts at 2,000 feet (610 m). Jumpers have to get their chute open within seconds and be careful not to hit anything as they fall!

Boenish's BASE Jump

Carl Boenish invented modern BASE jumping in 1978. He used skydiving equipment to jump off the El Capitan rock formation in California's Yosemite National Park. It's more than 3,000 feet (914 m) tall. Boenish died on a BASE jump in Norway in 1984.

BASE jumping from city buildings and in national parks is almost always illegal.

El Capitan

COMPETITION SKYDIVING

Some people are so crazy about skydiving that they want to be the best. There are 14 different skydiving events at the United States Parachute Association (USPA) National Championships. The USPA championships are the largest skydiving competition in the world. Individuals or groups make all kinds of jumps.

In formation skydiving, teams of 4, 8, 10, or even 16 race time as they create certain formations in the air before releasing their parachutes. Skydivers in the **freestyle** competition jump at 13,000 feet (3,962 m) and do gymnastics and even dance moves while falling.

This formation skydiving team performs a spectacular stunt in midair.

This skydiver must steer his way around objects in the water to win a canopy piloting competition.

Canopy Piloting

One of the coolest skydiving competitions to watch from the ground is canopy piloting. The best skydiving athletes fly special parachutes through courses over water or over the ground. They may be traveling at speeds of 75 miles (121 km) per hour. There are different events for the fastest, the longest, and the most exact, or accurate, jumps.

FIXING MISTAKES

Every sport has its dangers, but skydiving involves a lot more risk than riding a bike. A free fall can easily go wrong if the jumpmaster thinks the skydiver is ready to leave the plane when he or she isn't. When a skydiver is pulled into the air by the jumpmaster too soon, it's hard for the skydiver to move into the right position to make a safe dive.

Jumpmasters suggest pulling the rip cord and ending the free fall when the unexpected happens in the air. This includes when a skydiver can't gain control of their position, if they don't know how high off the ground they are, or if they lose their jumpmaster in the air.

Unexpected Landings

Most skydiving landings end safely without any problems. However, winds can blow skydivers off course so they land in trees or around power lines. Some skydivers even land in water. Experts recommend that a skydiver release the parachute the second their feet hit water, so that it'll be carried away by the wind and won't fall on them.

An altimeter like this one tells skydivers and jumpmasters how high they are, so they know when to pull their rip cord to let out the parachute.

INJURIES AND FATALITIES

Skydiving can be safe with good training and practice, but jumping out of an airplane has its share of injuries and even fatalities. Most accidents happen because of human error.

For example, how the parachute is packed is very important. Some people get tangled up in the lines that connect them to the parachute. The parachute must release smoothly when the rip cord is pulled to avoid this. Also, the rip cord must be pulled at the right time, not too soon and not too late. Problems can be avoided with careful planning each and every dive.

What Are the Odds?

In 2012, the USPA reported 915 skydiving injuries out of more than 3.1 million jumps. That's roughly three injuries per 10,000 skydives. According to the National Safety Council, a person is much more likely to be killed getting struck by lightning! The information in the chart on the next page comes from the USPA.

US SKYDIVING FATALITIES

year	skydiving fatalities	estimated jumps
2012	19	3.1 million
2011	25	3.1 million
2010	21	3.0 million
2009	16	3.0 million
2008	30	2.6 million
2007	18	2.5 million
2006	21	2.5 million
2005	27	2.6 million
2004	21	2.6 million
2003	25	2.6 million
2002	33	2.6 million
2001	35	2.6 million
2000	32	2.7 million

JOE KITTINGER'S HISTORIC DIVE

Higher jumps and faster speeds increase the danger for skydivers. US Air Force captain Joe Kittinger holds the record for the longest free fall. On August 16, 1960, Kittinger used a special high-altitude balloon to climb to 102,800 feet (31,333 m). At that height, he needed more than the usual skydiving gear. He needed oxygen and a special **pressurized** suit!

This jump set world records for the highest open-basket balloon ascent and the longest parachute descent. Kittinger's jump wasn't for thrills or honors but to gather information for the US space program.

Joe Kittinger

Besides oxygen, skydivers above 63,000 feet (19,202 m) need a pressurized suit like Kittinger wore.

The Troposphere and the Stratosphere

Joe Kittinger had to pass through two layers of the atmosphere on his way down—the stratosphere and the troposphere. In the stratosphere, a person's blood can boil without a pressurized suit! In the troposphere, the air can be as cold as −70°F (−57°C).

"FEARLESS FELIX" BAUMGARTNER

"Fearless Felix" Baumgartner's 2012 skydive was both higher and faster than Kittinger's. He actually went supersonic! That means he traveled faster than the speed of sound.

On October 14, 2012, Baumgartner jumped from a **capsule** about 128,100 feet (39,045 m) above Earth. That's more than 24 miles (39 km) high! The speed of sound at that height is about 690 miles (1,110 km) per hour. Baumgartner's fastest speed during his 9-minute fall was 843.6 miles (1,357.4 km) per hour! No one has ever fallen as fast as Felix Baumgartner wearing only a skydiving suit.

Beware of the Balloon

Even the balloons that carried up Kittinger and Baumgartner had their dangers. They were made of extremely thin material that might have been damaged under harsh conditions. Wind can blow a skydiver's balloon off course, too. Luckily, both skydivers lived to tell their tales!

Felix Baumgartner landed safely in New Mexico after his historic dive.

Felix Baumgartner's skydive was 7 years in the making. He and his team, which included Joe Kittinger, planned for every possibility they could. However, during his free fall, Baumgartner fell into a flat spin. This means his head and feet spun around the center of his body. There was a danger that he'd fall **unconscious**, that his brain could bleed, or even that his eyeballs would burst! Luckily, when Baumgartner reached higher air pressure, the denser air slowed him, and he regained control of his body.

Now that you know a bit about the thrilling world of skydiving, would you like to take the plunge?

Baumgartner, the BASE Jumper

Felix Baumgartner made a record-setting lowest BASE jump from the Christ the Redeemer statue in Rio de Janeiro, Brazil (at right). Not once, but twice, he set world records for the highest BASE jump, too. Once, Baumgartner landed inside a cave!

Baumgartner made his first skydive at age 16. He sharpened his skills in the Austrian military before becoming a skydiving professional.

GLOSSARY

altitude: height above sea level

antenna: a metal tool used to send and receive radio waves

capsule: a sealed container

drogue: a small parachute that is released before a larger one to slow an object

free fall: a descent through the air with an unopened parachute

freestyle: describing an event in which someone may use a style of their own choosing

gummed: something stuck to something else

license: official permission to do something

parachute: a specially shaped piece of cloth that collects air to slow something down

pressurized: having normal air pressure in a space in order to stay safe when outside air pressure falls

rig: special equipment organized in a small space

rip cord: a cord that, when pulled, opens a parachute

unconscious: unable to see, hear, or sense what is happening because of accident or injury

FOR MORE INFORMATION

BOOKS

Labrecque, Ellen. *Sky Surfing.* Mankato, MN: Child's World, 2012.

Mattern, Joanne. *Skydiving.* Vero Beach, FL: Rourke Publishing, 2010.

Young, Jeff C. *Pulling the Rip Cord: Skydiving.* Edina, MN: ABDO Publishing, 2011.

WEBSITES

Born to Fly
www.redbullstratos.com/about-felix/
Learn more about Felix Baumgartner's great feat.

United States Parachute Association (USPA)
www.uspa.org
Learn all about the thrills and dangers of skydiving on the USPA website with articles, charts, and more.

INDEX